Simple Gifts

DAILY REFLECTIONS FOR
Advent

Diane M. Houdek

franciscan
media
Cincinnati, Ohio

Scripture passages have been taken from *New Revised Standard Version Bible,* copyright ©1989 by the Division of Christian Education of the National Council of the Churches of Christ in the U.S.A., and used by permission. All rights reserved. Quotes from Pope Francis are © 2013–2015, Libreria Editrice Vaticana and used by permission. All rights reserved.

Cover and book design by Mark Sullivan

ISBN 978-1-63253-272-5

Published by Franciscan Media
28 W. Liberty St.
Cincinnati, OH 45202
www.FranciscanMedia.org

Printed in the United States of America.
Printed on acid-free paper.
18 19 20 21 22   5 4 3 2 1

CONTENTS

When the Season Takes a Detour

A voice cries out:
"In the wilderness prepare the way of the LORD,
   make straight in the desert a highway for our God.
Every valley shall be lifted up,
   and every mountain and hill be made low;
the uneven ground shall become level,
   and the rough places a plain."

—ISAIAH 40:3–4

*A*dvent calendars have become quite a commodity in secular culture. They're far more sophisticated than the simple paper and cardboard doors with hidden pictures for each day that I had as a child. Chocolate is a popular daily treat, but I've also seen ads for gin, whiskey, and single malt scotch Advent calendars. There are coloring books with a design for every day leading up to Christmas and for the last several years I've knit scarves with a daily lace motif accompanied by a meditation.

For many people, Advent is synonymous with counting down the days of December from the first to the twenty-fifth.

Advent is far more than just preparation for Christmas. It has beauty and inspiration in its own right. It's a fresh start, an invitation to enter into the silence and the mystery of whatever is waiting to be born or reborn in our lives. Paradoxically it's an invitation to slow down, to come away to the quiet, at the very time our daily lives are immersed in activity—shopping, parties, baking, cleaning. It's a reminder that the promise of Christ is "already but not yet." The Church begins a new liturgical year. The Scriptures for the season describe the apocalyptic end of time and the Second Coming, but they also remind us of the minutely precious details of the First Coming.

Advent is a time of turning, because as Christians we are always in a process of conversion, turning away from sin and toward the light of Christ. We are called to prepare a place for Jesus in our hearts and our lives in the same way the people of the Hebrew Scriptures longed for the Messiah and in the same way Mary and Joseph made preparations for the birth of their first child. Life as we know it is going to change if we live Advent well.

The call of Advent is clear. From both the prophet Isaiah and John the Baptist, we hear, "Make straight in the desert a highway for our God." Isaiah was writing to the people exiled far from their homeland. John the Baptist was talking to people who had lost their way in a tangle of politics and religion. In our own lives, we hear this call as well. We all have some roadwork to do in our souls. We might say Advent is construction season.

Many years ago, an Advent reconciliation service turned my life around and set me on an incredible journey toward the life I'm now living. This might be why Advent has always held a special place in my heart and in my spirituality. People have asked me what it was that made such a difference, hoping to create a service in their own parishes that would change people's lives. But I know that the truth is the ritual only created the opportunity for the spirit to appear. My life had been broken open by stress and exhaustion and in that place of vulnerability, simple words took root and began to grow: "You are loved and lovable simply because God has created you." Once I began exploring the truth of that sentence, my life changed. I stopped trying to prove myself and my worth. I let myself love and be loved. I discovered a new and renewed creativity and confidence.

I had been on the edges of church life between childhood and my young adult years, but suddenly I wanted to go deeper into the faith I had taken for granted. What had seemed like a revelation out of the blue I now discovered throughout the Scriptures. The writings of the prophets and the message of the gospel tell us again and again that we are loved by God, that we're held in the palm of God's hand. The story of the storm at sea tells us that God can calm the storms of our lives—and if the storm continues to rage around us for whatever reason, then our loving God holds us and calms us and keeps us safe in his care. In time, I was able to see how that simple phrase applies to everyone and everything. We are loved and loveable simply because God created us. All of creation pours forth from the eternal love of God, and it is marvelous in his eyes.

The change didn't happen overnight or even in a season or a year. It's an ongoing conversion that I expect will last a lifetime. Anyone who has ever struggled with spiritual or psychological healing (and isn't that everyone on some level?) knows that the initial revelation or insight is only the beginning. But each year when Advent rolls around on the calendar, I remember and I reflect and I nurture that belief until it grows stronger and brighter and more reliable. The peaks are a little less intense, perhaps, but the valleys aren't quite as deep and dark.

Pope Francis has proven to be a trusted guide in dealing with the stress of the Christmas season and the anxiety of daily life in general. In his apostolic exhortation Rejoice and Be Glad, he puts his finger on the dangers of a frenetic quest for happiness:

> The presence of constantly new gadgets, the excitement of travel and an endless array of consumer goods at times leave no room for God's voice to be heard. We are overwhelmed by words, by superficial pleasures and by an increasing din, filled not by joy but rather by the discontent of those whose lives have lost meaning. How can we fail to realize the need to stop this rat race and to recover the personal space needed to carry on a heartfelt dialogue with God? Finding that space may prove painful but it is always fruitful. Sooner or later,

we have to face our true selves and let the Lord enter. This may not happen unless "we see ourselves staring into the abyss of a frightful temptation, or have the dizzying sensation of standing on the precipice of utter despair, or find ourselves completely alone and abandoned." In such situations, we find the deepest motivation for living fully our commitment to our work (#29).

We are constantly surrounded by advertising in a growing variety of forms. Ads creep into nearly everything we do. And this ramps up even more during the weeks leading up to Christmas. Advent invites us to take a break from the deluge of ads and seek something deeper and more lasting than the latest electronics or the best deal on that kitchen appliance that everyone needs this year. Advent invites us to seek a sense of peace and wholeness in our hearts and in our daily lives. If we do that even in small ways this year, we will have an immeasurable gift to share with our loved ones and possibly even with our world.

Advent doesn't make the same demands on us that Lent does. It begins quietly, with the lighting of the first candle on the Advent wreath. As the days grow shorter in the Northern Hemisphere, we move to a place of increasing light both indoors and in our hearts. Instead of adding more things to do and more challenges to meet in an already busy time, Advent calls us to rest, to step back, to learn to appreciate the small events and simple gifts that flow through our days. My hope is that these reflections will remind you of the life-changing truths that lie deep within your own heart. Wisdom from Scripture, from saints and spiritual writers, and from everyday life offers that opportunity to learn more about ourselves and the God who loved us enough to become one of us and share our journey.

Let this Advent be a simple gift you give to yourself!

Slow Down

> This is the surprising greatness of God, of a God who is full of surprises and who loves surprises: let us always keep alive the desire for and trust in God's surprises!
>
> —POPE FRANCIS, HOMILY, OCTOBER 1, 2016

*P*ope Francis frequently refers to our "God of surprises." I know the truth of this from my own life, but I also know that the surprise isn't always pleasant, at least not at first. This is never more clear to me than during the big seasons of the liturgical year. I plan my prayer routines and spiritual reading and other activities for the season, and then I discover that God has other plans for me.

Advent 2017 was no exception. I had prepared beforehand. I had a least four Advent calendars lined up: an old one from Starbucks that I refilled with Dove chocolates, a tea calendar from a local tea shop, and two Advent yarn kits. I had been feeling a bit under the weather since Thanksgiving but determined to push through it and stick to my to-do list and my plans. I was getting short of breath and attributed it to not enough exercise and being out of shape. I thought maybe Advent would give me the impetus I needed to start an exercise routine. So added to the physical struggle, I was also beating myself up for not taking better care of myself.

By Monday of the first week of Advent, I ended up in the emergency room with acute respiratory failure. My immune system was attacking my lungs and I had been too busy and preoccupied to recognize the early warning signs. Overwhelmed by commitments and things to do, I brushed aside my health concerns until I could no longer ignore them.

I later said to my spiritual director, "Does God have to put me in the hospital to get my attention?" He laughed and said, "Apparently he does!" I was joking, but only a bit. God doesn't bring sickness and suffering into our lives. But he is there when we finally hit bottom and realize that our strength isn't limitless and our need for help and healing can't be ignored. Too often we're not aware of that divine presence until an illness or accident forces us to stop and reflect.

Our bodies sometimes know better than our minds what

we really need. And these days it's the rare person who won't benefit from a loving reminder to slow down. From experience, I know that the more I say, "I don't have time to rest," the more urgent it is that I take heed of that reminder. For this first week of Advent, we'll reflect on the call to slow our pace until we are walking in God's rhythm instead of hurrying to keep up with a fast-paced world.

We don't know how to rest and relax anymore. Picture an overtired toddler fighting a much-needed nap. This is a good image for many of us as we push ourselves through days filled with too much activity and too much stress. Part of the problem is that too often the work we do takes place mostly in our brains and on our computers. We are mentally but not physically tired. People who work in physically demanding jobs perhaps have a better awareness of the body's need for rest. I think my parents and grandparents were much better than I am at balancing work and rest.

But this isn't solely a twenty-first-century phenomenon. As far back as the beginning of the Hebrew Scriptures, God had to command one day of rest for the Chosen People. Left to ourselves, like toddlers we will keep going until we drop in our tracks. One of my favorite quotes from Isaiah talks about how quiet trust and rest will lead to salvation. It wasn't until I found the quote in its full context that I understood how much we resist the very thing we most need:

> For thus said the LORD God, the Holy One of Israel:
> In returning and rest you shall be saved;
>   in quietness and in trust shall be your strength.
> But you refused and said,
>   "No! We will flee upon horses"—
> therefore you shall flee!—Isaiah 30:15–16

We rely a great deal—probably too much—on our own efforts. We become convinced that we're indispensable and irreplaceable. We don't realize that it's OK to ask for help—or at least allow ourselves to take a day off and return to the task with renewed energy.

Reflect this week on how God gets your attention. If you haven't noticed God trying to get through to you, take a little extra time for prayer and ask what you might be missing.

This is the perfect time to start a new prayer routine or revive an old one. The Liturgy of the Hours, the official daily prayer of the church, begins anew on the First Sunday of Advent with Week One, Day One. Advent is also a lovely time to spend with Mary, the Mother of God. Make a commitment to pray the rosary each day of the season.

DAY ONE

The Waiting Time

Yet O Lord, you are our Father;
we are the clay and you the potter:
we are all the work of your hands.

—Isaiah 64:8

*F*rom God shaping Adam from the ground through prophets such as Isaiah and Jeremiah to Jesus making a paste from mud to cure a blind man, the image of God as potter, working with the clay of the earth, reminds us that we have the humblest of beginnings but a divine spirit and destiny. Knowing that we are the work of God's hands should reassure us when we question our physical attributes. It should also encourage us to take better care of our bodies, much as we would treat a precious ceramic vase or even a practical piece of kitchen pottery.

A great deal of time and patience goes into creating something from clay. The intuitive and creative skill of the potter works to shape the clay but much can happen in the drying and glazing process. And a piece is only finished after it's gone through the high heat of the kiln that changes its very composition and molecular structure. For a human potter, waiting in between stages takes a great deal of patience. Beginners often worry about hidden imperfections and cracks that can destroy a piece during firing. Fortunately, our divine potter has all the skill and patience needed to guide us to completion.

We might think of patience as trust through time. And our perception of time changes as we grow older. Remember what this time of year felt like when you were a child? It seemed as though Christmas would never get here. Children live so much in the present moment that it's hard to get them to understand the passage of time and the need to wait. As we get older, though, it seems as though time moves faster and faster. We look back on our teenage and young adult years and wonder when we found time to hang out with our friends, to play games (card, board, video—the medium changes but the pastime doesn't). We might think it's our work and family responsibilities, and that's part of it, but even people who have retired say that they find it hard to find time for all that they want to do.

Only at the very end of our lives do we again find time hanging heavy around us. If infirmity and illness keep us from doing the things we love, the days may feel endless and the nights even more so. Instead of having to slow down, we need to remind ourselves that we're in the perfect time and place for long and leisurely conversations with God.

TAKE A DEEP BREATH

Hanukkah and the beginning of Advent coincide this year. The tradition of not working while the lights of the menorah burn is a good example for us. Too often prayer becomes one more thing that we have to do in order to cross it off some spiritual list. Slow down and take time for a real prayer encounter with God. We might pray along with our Jewish brothers and sisters, "Blessed are you, Lord God, King of the Universe, who has brought us to this holy season." As they kindle the lights of the menorah, we light the first candle on our Advent wreaths.

A SIMPLE GIFT

Today is the day to get out your Advent wreath, or buy or make a new one. It can be as simple as a green wreath with four candles set within it—three purple and one pink. I've used the traditional tapers but I've also used votive candles in glass containers that burn longer without dripping. This is the main symbol of this season when we celebrate the light that comes into our darkness.

DAY TWO
Our Busy Lives

Beware that your hearts don't become drowsy from carousing and drunkenness and the anxieties of daily life.

—Luke 21:34 (NAB)

*S*ometimes religious people can get carried away with separating Advent from the Christmas season, refusing invitations to pre-Christmas parties and banning all Christmas music and decorations until December 25. This can especially be an issue for people deeply involved in parish liturgies and activities. Advent begins to feel like a penitential season with no celebration allowed. But life rarely fits into the neat compartments of an IKEA shelving unit. We can strive to hold onto the quiet withdrawal of the ideal Advent, but when that means refusing the hospitality of another's invitation, we might need to reconsider our commitments.

We take seriously the words of Jesus in Luke's Gospel when he warns against "carousing and drunkenness." But he also warns against "the anxieties of daily life." We know that especially in Luke's Gospel, Jesus was fond of a dinner party or a celebration with friends. And it's from Luke that we hear the story of Mary and Martha. When Martha, busy about the many tasks of hospitality, asks Jesus to make her sister, sitting at his feet, help in the kitchen, he tells her, "Martha, Martha, you are busy and anxious about many things. Mary has chosen the better part."

It's so easy to get wrapped up in the many tasks of this season of preparation. Cleaning, cooking, shopping, wrapping packages, cleaning some more, baking, doing dishes, going on one more shopping excursion. As so often happens during busy times, we find ourselves going to bed late, getting up early, grabbing fast food on the go, skipping a workout at the gym because we don't have time, and generally not taking good care of ourselves. Then we go to parties where we eat too much rich, sweet food, and drink one too many alcoholic beverages and the downward spiral continues.

TAKE A DEEP BREATH

Sit quietly for five or ten minutes today. Pay attention to your breathing. Hear Jesus say, "You are busy and anxious about many things." You know what those anxieties are. As you breathe in calm reassurance, breathe out those anxieties and turn them over to the Lord.

A SIMPLE GIFT

Ask your body and your spirit what they need at this time. It might be rest. Then again it might be more exercise. Our needs change throughout our lives and we don't always pay attention to that. Take a walk. Take a nap. Do both. Cancel an engagement and stay home for the evening. Or resist the pull of the recliner and Netflix and go to dinner with a good friend. The main thing is to take time to ask yourself in any given moment if what you're doing is really what you need or if another choice would be better. Then make the better choice, choose the better part.

DAY THREE
Don't Forget to Breathe

Then the LORD God formed man from the dust of the ground, and breathed into his nostrils the breath of life; and the man became a living being.

—GENESIS 2:7

I have an Apple watch and one of the built-in apps is called Breathe. It can be set up with notifications to remind you to take time for mindful breathing. I can't tell you how many times I've yelled at it, "I don't have time to breathe right now!!" Even when what I mean is "I can't stop what I'm doing and close my eyes and do one to three minutes of deep breathing." But sometimes it hits me that at times I do become so busy and stressed that I don't take time to breathe.

Irony of ironies, while I was lying in the ER last December, my watched pinged and said, "A minute of deep breathing can clear your mind and help you focus." Yes, thank you, I'm on fourteen liters of oxygen at the moment! My mind should be clear as a bell!

There's something a little bit crazy about using our technology to remind us of the simplest functions. I joke that my phone and my watch remind me to breathe, stand, and drink water. But it's a sign of how often we forget to do these things. And the many mindfulness apps available for our smartphones and computers can be a great help in changing our habits and routines.

My watch isn't wrong. A few minutes of deep breathing is an easy and refreshing way to take a break, clear my mind, check my body for stress-related aches, and get a renewed start on the tasks of the day. Long before we relied on technology, spiritual teachers in all the great religious traditions developed exercises that incorporate breathing into a prayer practice. It clears our spirits and opens a path for God's loving voice to break through.

TAKE A DEEP BREATH

Commit yourself to just five minutes to sit silently with God, feeling the breath of the Spirit with each breath you take. You might want to say a prayer with each breath: "Come, Lord

Jesus," "Emmanuel, God with us," or "Creator of the stars of night" are good reminders of this season of Advent. The traditional Jesus prayer—"Lord Jesus Christ, have mercy on me"—is a good way to focus your breathing. In the coming days, we will suggest Scripture passages as well.

A SIMPLE GIFT

One of the great blessings of technology is the easy availability of a wide variety of daily prayers. Through email, smartphone apps, and websites, we can find new ways to access the great spiritual riches of our tradition. Spend some time today looking for something that will enhance your prayer time during this Advent season. And if you're not into technology, there's no shortage of traditional paper resources.

DAY FOUR

Glorious Abundance for the Senses

On this mountain the LORD of hosts will make for all
    peoples
a feast of rich food, a feast of well-aged wines,
of rich food filled with marrow, of well-aged wines
    strained clear.

—ISAIAH 25:6

*E*very culture has special holiday foods and this becomes a big part of our experience of the festive season. We immerse ourselves in a sensual celebration of Advent and Christmas. Instead of being overwhelmed by this, let yourself take time to notice and truly appreciate the sights and sounds, aromas and tastes of the season.

For me, music is the first sign of the season. I like to start with the Windham Hill Winter Solstice collections and George Winston's *December*. They don't scream "CHRISTMAS!!!" but they instantly evoke the sounds of the season, partly because I've made them part of my yearly observance. An instrumental rendition of "O Come, O Come Emmanuel" or the "Carol of the Bells" begins to seep quietly into my consciousness. Collections by the St. Louis Jesuits, Marty Haugen, and David Haas bring the Scriptures of the season to life and allow a quiet reflection on the liturgical side of the season. "Advent Lessons and Carols" from the Anglican tradition is another of my staples. For many people, the season isn't complete without Handel's "Messiah." And many people prefer the familiar Christmas carols to put them in the spirit. Often our musical choices take us back to what spoke to us of Christmas in our childhood years or in other formative times.

I also wait for the first taste of eggnog and then the aroma of Christmas cookies baking in the oven. My sister makes special candy for Christmas and I love it when a box of goodies arrives in the mail. I can taste the love that goes into it. There's no reason these things can't happen at other times of the year. But connecting them with Advent and Christmas somehow makes them seem special. Like eating seasonally with the local harvest, we appreciate things more when we don't have them all the time.

When I was a child, one of the first things that happened was the appearance of the box of Christmas books to replace the books I read (or was read to) the rest of the year. Old favorites and a few new ones were very much part of my Christmas tradition and I now have my own collection of Advent and Christmas reading.

TAKE A DEEP BREATH

As you practice your breathing today, reflect on these words from Psalm 23:

The LORD is my shepherd, I shall not want.

He makes me lie down in green pastures;

he leads me beside still waters;

he restores my soul.

A SIMPLE GIFT

Make an Advent/Christmas playlist. Music is a big part of most of our experiences of Christmas. The right music can be a perfect background for a quiet appreciation of Advent. Everyone has different taste in music; use what works for you.

Check Your Foundation

Everyone then who hears these words of mine and acts on them will be like a wise man who built his house on rock. The rain fell, the floods came, and the winds blew and beat on that house, but it did not fall, because it had been founded on rock. And everyone who hears these words of mine and does not act on them will be like a foolish man who built his house on sand. The rain fell, and the floods came, and the winds blew and beat against that house, and it fell—and great was its fall!

—MATTHEW 7:24–27

*J*esus uses the metaphor of building a house on a solid foundation to describe those who hear and act on the word of God. His story sounds a bit silly on the surface. Who would build a house on shifting sand? We would never make this mistake in our actual homes, and yet we do it so often in our spiritual and emotional lives. It's easy to be pulled and pushed about by the next new thing and we don't always take time to anchor it to our core beliefs. We buy into the latest self-help craze and forget that our help comes from God. Sudden tragedy or disaster can threaten to knock us off our foundation or knock that foundation out from under us. No people or institutions are as solid and dependable as God.

Advent reminds us that the One who has come into the world and is always coming into our lives in new ways is the source of our salvation. We don't need novelty and "magic bullet" solutions to our concerns. We simply need to return again and again to the rock-solid foundation of our lives: God and God alone. The mystery of the Incarnation is that by entering into our time and into our world, Jesus can show us the way to the gift that is beyond all time.

It can be hard to remember this when the storms of life hit unexpectedly. Using the season of Advent as a time to cultivate a deeper prayer life will help us with our spiritual emergency preparedness kit. We will have deeply rooted routines that can kick in when powers we depend on fail—as they all will at one time or another.

TAKE A DEEP BREATH

Reflect on these words from the prophet Isaiah as you sit quietly with your breathing today:

> Trust in the LORD forever,
>> for in the LORD God
>> you have an everlasting rock. (Isaiah 26:4)

A SIMPLE GIFT

It's easy to take on too much at this time of year and forget why we're doing what we're doing. We find ourselves overwhelmed, drowning in anxiety and debt. Take a look at your to-do list. It has a way of getting out of control this time of year. Learn to say no to some things so you can be fully present to those things to which you say yes.

DAY SIX

Hear the Word of God

On that day the deaf shall hear
  the words of a scroll,
and out of their gloom and darkness
  the eyes of the blind shall see.
The meek shall obtain fresh joy in the LORD,
   and the neediest people shall exult in the Holy One
    of Israel.
For the tyrant shall be no more,
  and the scoffer shall cease to be;
  all those alert to do evil shall be cut off.

—ISAIAH 29:18–20

*T*he prophet Isaiah is the voice and spirit of the Advent season. In the eighth century before Christ was born, his words encouraged a people dejected and torn from their homes by soldiers of a foreign power. The people of Israel were carried off to Assyria, exiled from their homeland, driven out of the Promised Land. While God's prophets, including Isaiah, had warned them time and time again that this would happen, until they were living the reality of the exile, they didn't see the need to change their ways. But once the worst had happened, he changed his tone and his words brought comfort and hope to an afflicted people. He continued to call them to change their lives and turn again to their God, but he did it with gentleness and encouragement, with reminders of how very much God loved them, even in the midst of their suffering.

At different times in our lives, we find ourselves beaten down by circumstances—some beyond our control and some the consequence of bad choices on our part. We're embarrassed by the number of times people have warned us that we were going the wrong way. We feel consumed by regret and remorse. At times such as these, we need to hear the word of God through the prophet Isaiah, reminding us that God is merciful, that God loves us just as we are, that in spite of our weakness and sin, God is always ready to welcome us home, to bring us back to level ground.

If you've reached one of these valleys during this holiday season, don't beat yourself up for the way you're feeling.

Remember that our resolutions to do better, our commitment to repentance and turning our lives around, all happen with God's help.

TAKE A DEEP BREATH

There's a saying that prophets afflict the comfortable and comfort the afflicted. For today's prayer, let yourself hear deeply these familiar words from the prophet Isaiah:

Comfort, O comfort my people,
  says your God. (Isaiah 40:1)

As the word of God becomes part of our breathing, we are more likely to recall these words when we need them.

A SIMPLE GIFT

Do we let ourselves be tyrannized by unreasonable expectations? What's truly essential for your celebration of this season? What are you doing because you've always done it or because you think someone else expects it? If you enjoy something, by all means keep doing it. If it's a burden, consider letting go of it.

DAY SEVEN

A DIY Christmas?

A shoot shall come out from the stock of Jesse,
  and a branch shall grow out of his roots.
The spirit of the LORD shall rest on him,
  the spirit of wisdom and understanding,
  the spirit of counsel and might,
  the spirit of knowledge and the fear of the LORD.
His delight shall be in the fear of the LORD.

—ISAIAH 11:1–3

Other people much wiser (and perhaps more organized) than me start making Christmas gifts during the summer and have lovely handmade gifts for their loved ones on December 25. For these people, a handmade Christmas is a lovely, peaceful experience, one that I admire but can't seem to emulate.

My nephew's wife used to laugh at me because sometime in mid-November I would come up with an awesome idea for making all my Christmas gifts that year. Once it was going to be sets of notepaper and greeting cards for the family with images from our summer cottage. Another time it was going to be knitted gifts for everyone. Of course, I never allowed enough time and the great ideas faded away, replaced by a desperate trip to the store in late December to find appropriate gifts.

If you're a crafty person, it's hard to resist the urge to have a homemade Christmas. Magazines and Pinterest boards are filled with fun and creative ideas. Parents get sucked into making elaborate seasonal treats for their children's school parties. When these ideas make us stressful and anxious, or we find ourselves running to multiple stores looking for the right shape pretzels, it's time to take a step back and ask if it's really worth the effort. What started out as a way to make the season less commercial suddenly becomes anything but simple.

The answer isn't "do it" or "don't do it." It is, rather, pay attention to what's right for you and your family this year. And don't let yourself be swayed by external expectations, whether it's people you know or those tempting ideas in social media. Trust that you know what's best for your circumstances. Hear the words of Isaiah: "This is the way. Walk in it when you would turn to the right or left."

I'm still planning to make an elaborate knitted wreath for my door. Every year I get out the yarn and the pattern but I've made peace with only finishing a few knitted ivy leaves and mistletoe berries. I enjoy the process and I know it will get done someday—or it won't. My celebration of Christmas doesn't depend on it.

TAKE A DEEP BREATH

This quote from Isaiah could help you hold onto the healthy choices and plans you're making for the season. If you haven't made those plans yet, there's still time.

> And when you turn to the right or when you turn to
> the left, your ears shall hear a word behind you, saying,
> "This is the way; walk in it." (Isaiah 30:21)

A SIMPLE GIFT

If you want to get away from the big box stores but know that a DIY Christmas isn't going to happen, look into some middle ground alternatives. Shop at local small businesses. Support the many craft fairs held in your area to raise money for various groups and charities. Buy from independent artisans on sites such as Etsy. You'll find unique and interesting gifts for your families and friends and you have the added bonus of doing good in the process.

Simplify

For it was you who formed my inward parts;
  you knit me together in my mother's womb.
I praise you, for I am fearfully and wonderfully made.
  Wonderful are your works;
that I know very well.
  My frame was not hidden from you,
when I was being made in secret,
    intricately woven in the depths of the earth.

—PSALM 139:13–15

My friends and family all know that I am an obsessive knitter. No matter where I am, if I have a few minutes to wait, I take out my knitting. It fills what might be empty moments with color, texture, and pattern. It keeps my hands busy so my mind is free to wander or focus as needed. There's a meme going around among knitters that shows a nineteenth-century painting of a young girl knitting with the caption, "The original fidget-spinner."

The first time I ever had to be admitted to the hospital for a bronchoscopy, my primary care doctor did the preadmission tests and told me to go home and collect what I needed (I think his actual words were "whatever chargers you need") and then check in at the hospital. I made sure I had my laptop to keep up with work and several knitting projects. I joked that if I'd known they would make me wear a hospital gown the whole time, I would have had room for another project instead of a change of clothes. If I had to be in the hospital, I might as well make good use of the time.

Last year, though, I was completely unprepared. When you go to the ER in a rescue squad, you don't have the luxury of planning. I grabbed my phone and one simple scarf project. No iPad, no laptop, no work projects. The whole focus of my life for almost a week was breathing and breathing out. That's about as simple as it gets! As I began to feel better, I asked the hospital's volunteer coordinator for some yarn to make something for their prayer shawl ministry. But even that was secondary to my main occupation of breathing in and breathing out, first with oxygen and then gradually on my own.

We fill our lives and our calendars with more than we can do in twenty-four hours and we do that for days on end. Reluctant to cross anything off, we simply push tasks to the next day and the next. Often we accumulate possessions with the same disregard for space and clarity. Many of us struggle with letting go of the things in our lives, often because those things hold memories of our past and of beloved friends and family. Advent calls us to simplify our lives and our homes so we can focus on what really matters: being aware of the Spirit of God breathing within and around us.

As we begin the second week of Advent this year, we hear the call of John the Baptist to turn our lives around, to let go of those things that keep us too far away from God's presence. He preached a fierce and compelling message to people who had lost their way. But he also brought the message home to them in ways that spoke to the uniqueness of their way of life.

> And the crowds asked him, "What then should we do?" In reply he said to them, "Whoever has two coats must share with anyone who has none; and whoever has food must do likewise." Even tax-collectors came

to be baptized, and they asked him, "Teacher, what should we do?" He said to them, "Collect no more than the amount prescribed for you." Soldiers also asked him, "And we, what should we do?" He said to them, "Do not extort money from anyone by threats or false accusation, and be satisfied with your wages."

We have a tendency to live "all-or-nothing" lives, especially when we're trying to make changes and become better people. We swing from one extreme to the other and forget that temperance, too, is a virtue.

The Work of Our Hands

For God has ordered that every high mountain and the
    everlasting hills be made low
    and the valleys filled up, to make level ground,
    so that Israel may walk safely in the glory of God.
The woods and every fragrant tree
    have shaded Israel at God's command.
For God will lead Israel with joy,
    in the light of his glory,
    with the mercy and righteousness that come from
    him.

—BARUCH 5:7–9

*L*ast week we heard Jeremiah compare God to a potter. We
know from the gospels that Jesus worked with his foster father,
who was a carpenter (or a stonemason). St. Francis advised
his brothers to work with their hands as a way of staying
connected to the humble, simple things of the earth. Many
of our Christmas traditions pull us into this kind of tactile

creativity. It might be baking or making decorations or writing cards to distant friends and family. In a world that too often relies on mass-produced, cheaply made commodities, hand-made treasures still stand out.

The prophet Baruch reminds us that all of creation, including but not limited to human beings, has come from the creative hand of God. In using our hands creatively, we share in the creative impulse of God. We put more of ourselves into the work of our hands and that becomes an important part of the special gifts we give and the meals we prepare. These things we make don't need to be either elaborate or impressive. If we worry too much about making an impression, we lose the simplicity and the beauty of the gesture. We allow our anxieties and our pride to rob us of the simple joy of making and giving. We lose that connection with the God who created us and breathes life into us each and every day.

TAKE A DEEP BREATH

As you take time to breathe deeply in prayer today, look with appreciation at your hands and reflect on the many things they do—working, playing, loving, creating. Let the phrase "I am God's work of art" run through your mind as you breathe. It comes from this passage in Paul's letter to the Ephesians:

> For by grace you have been saved through faith, and this is not your own doing; it is the gift of God—not the result of works, so that no one may boast. For we are what he has made us, created in Christ Jesus for good works, which God prepared beforehand to be our way of life. (Ephesians 2:8–10)

A SIMPLE GIFT

A minimalism movement has arisen in response to an increasingly complex technological society and the excesses of our consumption-driven culture. One manifestation of this is a renewed interest in pen-and-paper planning and journaling. People are taking time away from their phones and tablets and rediscovering the tactile experience of writing by hand. Working by hand can slow us down and give us a greater appreciation for the task we're doing. You might want to write at least some of your Christmas cards by hand this year, even if it's just a short note. Or you might want to write out your Christmas shopping list, carefully pairing each person with an appropriate gift.

DAY TWO
The Beauty of Simplicity

The wilderness and the dry land shall be glad,
   the desert shall rejoice and blossom;
like the crocus it shall blossom abundantly,
   and rejoice with joy and singing.

—ISAIAH 35:1

*I*f you follow contemporary trends in design and interior decoration, you can't miss the move toward minimalism. As people find their lives becoming cluttered and out of control, they're drawn to an ideal of wide, clear spaces, polished wood, and large expanses of glass. I can appreciate the beauty of this, but it's not something to which I'm drawn. I like a little homey clutter. I like letting my eye rest on objects that carry memories and emotions and connections to places and people I've loved. I try to follow the advice of nineteenth-century philosopher and proponent of the Arts and Crafts movement William Morris who said, "Have nothing in your life that you don't know to be useful or believe to be beautiful."

Beauty rescues us from a drab utilitarian existence. Simplicity doesn't need to be stark and completely minimalist. Any time spent in nature, even in the depths of winter, shows us that our God is both prolific and even flamboyant in the colors and shapes and infinite variety of creation. Even the vast deserts and oceans are shifting displays of original beauty and blessing.

As you're cleaning and decorating this year, don't let the perfect be the enemy of the good. Trust your instincts and rely on your own tastes and preferences. If you want a single stem of holly for your centerpiece, go for it and let it reflect a single-hearted focus on God's grace. If you want every ornament you've inherited from parents, grandparents, and great-grandparents jostling for space on your tree, glory in the extravagance.

TAKE A DEEP BREATH

Do not remember the former things,
    or consider the things of old.
I am about to do a new thing;
    now it springs forth, do you not perceive it?

I will make a way in the wilderness
  and rivers in the desert. (Isaiah 43:18–19)

A SIMPLE GIFT

Before you start decorating for the holiday, take a day or two to put away the decorations you've been enjoying for the autumn months (or perhaps the eleven months since last Christmas). Clear and clean the surfaces in your living space and enjoy the emptiness and openness for a time. Let the simplicity offer you some rest and peace as you prepare for the coming feast. You might want to include flowering bulbs (amaryllis and narcissus are popular choices) or a Christmas cactus as part of your decorations to bring to mind Isaiah's hope-filled words about the desert blooming.

DAY THREE
Nothing Lasts Forever

A voice says, "Cry out!"
  And I said, "What shall I cry?"
All people are grass,
  their constancy is like the flower of the field.
The grass withers, the flower fades,
  when the breath of the LORD blows upon it;
  surely the people are grass.
The grass withers, the flower fades;
  but the word of our God will stand forever.

—ISAIAH 40:6–8

*E*very few years a new organizing and clutter-clearing trend makes the news. The latest one I've encountered is Swedish death-cleaning (*döstädning*). The underlying principle makes sense: From around age fifty, you should begin organizing your things and decluttering so that your children aren't stuck with the task after you're gone. I can appreciate this. When my mom died, we needed multiple large dumpsters to clear out her house, partly because she absorbed the household goods from several aging and deceased relatives. While this might seem to be more of a project for Lent, it can be a fruitful Advent pursuit as well. When we get out the boxes of Christmas decorations, often we find things at the bottom of the box or the back of the closet that never get pulled out. Not too long ago I found the flour-and-salt-clay diorama of a winter scene that I made in third grade. The plastic deer had a broken back leg and the clay itself was cracked in several places. I took a picture of it and let it go.

Sometimes we simply don't think about our possessions in this way. As long as we have room for them, we keep them stored away. But they no longer have any meaning for the person we've become and even if they might have an emotional attachment for us, they're not going to mean anything so significant to anyone else. If you're not ready to death-clean your whole house, this Advent start with the Christmas decorations. When you put them away in January, the boxes will be lighter and maybe your heart will be as well.

TAKE A DEEP BREATH

We sometimes mistake the transitory for permanent and vice versa. As you pay attention to your breathing today, reflect on these words from Isaiah. You might be surprised by the emotions that arise as part of your prayer.

The grass withers, the flower fades;
but the word of our God will stand for ever.
(Isaiah 40:8)

A SIMPLE GIFT

Emotions run high during the holidays and big gatherings don't lend themselves to serious discussions. But if this idea of anticipatory cleaning appeals to you, decide to find a time in the new year to talk with your children and close friends. If you know someone has expressed an interest in a precious possession and you're ready to let go of it, consider surprising them with it as a gift this Christmas. If you're not quite ready to let it go, make a point of telling them that it will come to them some day in the future.

DAY FOUR

Life Is Too Short

Those who wait for the LORD shall renew their strength,
  they shall mount up with wings like eagles,
they shall run and not be weary,
  they shall walk and not faint.

—ISAIAH 40:31

*S*implicity is not about being poor and deprived; rather it's about being filled with joy because our needs and wants are no longer consuming us. Too often we grasp at things when we're struggling with a feeling of emptiness within. We know that what's missing can't be replaced by things, but we fall into old habits and beliefs. As we grow older and more mature, as we repeat this cycle more times than we care to count, the message does begin to sink in. As we become more aware of what things truly give us pleasure and fulfillment, we can let the incidentals go.

The older we get, the less we need. It's somewhat ironic that we give older people in our lives completely useless trinkets

43

because there's nothing practical that they need or want. But they also don't need or want trinkets. Gift-giving can lose its meaning when it becomes a meaningless list of items to check off as they're purchased.

If you have older people in your life, think about ways you can give them the gift of loving time. Don't simply give them a gift card to a restaurant; include an invitation to make it a family dinner time. Offer to take them to a special event after the hectic holiday season is over and the winter days and nights stretch bleakly into early spring. Ask them if there's something they would like. If you're an older person, make suggestions to your children and grandchildren about what you would like.

TAKE A DEEP BREATH

Whatever age you are, this prayer can help focus your thoughts and bring peace to your heart:

> Grant me daily the grace of gratitude, to be thankful for all my many gifts, and so be freed from artificial needs, that I might lead a joyful, simple life. (Fr. Ed Hays)

A SIMPLE GIFT

A gift to a favorite charity can be a special way to honor someone that doesn't become a burden or even just a dust-catcher. Many organizations even have lovely gift cards that let the person know you've made a donation in their name. At a family gathering, take a few minutes and have each person suggest a favorite cause for future gift-giving occasions.

DAY FIVE

Love Is Always Greater than Things

Do not store up for yourselves treasures on earth,
where moth and rust consume and where thieves break
in and steal; but store up for yourselves treasures in
heaven, where neither moth nor rust consumes and
where thieves do not break in and steal. For where
your treasure is, there your heart will be also.

—MATTHEW 6:19–21

*T*ragedies have a way of showing us what really matters.
Losing everything in a house fire or flood is devastating. The
wildfires in the western United States have destroyed thou-
sands of acres and raged indiscriminately through homes and
businesses across the economic spectrum. Floods along the
eastern seaboard and tornadoes in the Midwest are a seasonal
reminder that nature doesn't pay attention to what's in its path.
But almost across the board, the response of people who lose
their material goods is simply thanksgiving for lives spared.
Homes can be rebuilt, possessions can be replaced.

Even more minor accidents take us by surprise. I woke up before dawn one morning to the sound of crashing glass. My first thought was my curio cabinet, but it turned out to be a wall shelf in the kitchen that held my spice jars and a variety of coffee mugs. First, I was immensely grateful that none of the dogs got hurt by the falling shelf. And I was ridiculously pleased that the damage to my mug collection was relatively minor. I set about cleaning up the mess and got on with the day.

There was a time when I would have been far more upset at the breakage and loss. It reminded me of when my first dog was a puppy and chewed up a Steiff zebra that had been a Christmas present from my dad. I was sad about the loss, but knew that the bond I had with my dog Bosch was more important than a stuffed animal, no matter how precious. I learned an important lesson that day that has stayed with me ever since.

TAKE A DEEP BREATH

The words of Isaiah continue to offer us comfort and stability in a life that can seem to have neither:

For I, the LORD your God,
  hold your right hand;
it is I who say to you, "Do not fear,
  I will help you." (Isaiah 41:13)

A SIMPLE GIFT

Accidents happen during this busy season. Baking treats and decorating the house can lead to spills and broken ornaments—even heirloom ones. Remember that the child or pet who was at fault is ultimately more important than the thing that got broke or the floor that needed to be cleaned.

DAY SIX

Everything We Want

Thus says the LORD,
  your Redeemer, the Holy One of Israel:
I am the LORD your God,
  who teaches you for your own good,
  who leads you in the way you should go.
O that you had paid attention to my commandments!
  Then your prosperity would have been like a river,
  and your success like the waves of the sea;
your offspring would have been like the sand,
  and your descendants like its grains;
their name would never be cut off
  or destroyed from before me.

—ISAIAH 48:17–19

*I*n the book *The Real Enjoyment of Living*, Rabbi Hyman Schachtel coined the often-quoted phrase, "Happiness is not having what you want, but wanting what you have." It's a good reminder at this time of year when we never quite lose the childish tendency to want everything we see advertised, even if it's just a momentary desire. People in the world of fiber often joke that money can't buy happiness, but it can buy yarn, which is almost the same thing. But we're all wise enough to know this isn't really true. Advent is a good time to reflect on the many gifts we already have, and even on the many material things that make our lives more pleasant and less difficult. But we don't have to be very far along in the spiritual life to understand that having more isn't going to fill an emptiness in our souls.

Contentment is a great gift that we don't always appreciate. It's not as rare as we might think. Instead of asking whether we're happy, perhaps we can get into the habit of asking how content we are. Contentment has in it an element of peace that's greatly needed in our lives and in our world today. And the more content we are with what we possess, the more likely we are to hold those things lightly and to give to those whose needs are greater and more genuine than our passing desires.

Notice Isaiah speaks of prosperity and success being like a river or the waves of the sea: infinite but constantly in motion. We are to hold our treasures lightly, knowing that they come from God.

TAKE A DEEP BREATH

Today you might want to add a variation to our familiar breathing prayer. Take a short (or long) walk and let these words of Psalm 25 be the refrain that guides your steps:

> Make me to know your ways, O LORD;
>   teach me your paths.
> Lead me in your truth, and teach me,
>   for you are the God of my salvation;
>   for you I wait all day long. (Psalm 25:4–5)

A SIMPLE GIFT

I have a deep respect for young parents I know who teach their children the invaluable lesson of giving to others. A few weeks before Christmas, they take the time to sort through old toys and give those that they've outgrown to thrift stores and other charitable giving organizations. Together as a family they select items for the parish giving tree. These children will grow into caring and giving adults because of these gentle lessons learned early and well. Make a special effort this year to give generously to those in need. It can be a side benefit of clearing away your own unneeded clutter or it can be an antidote to frenetic Christmas shopping.

DAY SEVEN

The Hardest Thing to Let Go

Come to me, all you that are weary and are carrying heavy burdens, and I will give you rest.

—MATTHEW 11:28

As we've been reflecting here on simplicity and as you look for new and creative ways to simplify your life, you might find yourself getting stuck over particular possessions or that one drawer in your desk where you're storing old letters. As you reminisce about Christmases past, there might be that year when family tension overshadowed the celebration that year. You either avoid thinking about it or it's all you can think about and you lose the memories of happier times. This might be the first Christmas without the presence of a dearly loved friend or family member.

We can become extreme minimalists, we can give away most of our possessions to the poor, we can simplify our external lives to the barest necessities, but the hardest thing to let go of might be the deeply emotional memories and conflicts in our past. The holidays often surface these difficulties. Advent offers us the opportunity each year to come to a place of peace and reconciliation with our past. Sometimes the issue is the loss of great happiness. Other times it's the looming presence of an unresolved struggle. These are the things that tie our inner lives into complex knots no matter how hard we work to simplify the surface.

TAKE A DEEP BREATH

Sometimes it helps to begin with our goal in mind. As we take our need for letting go to prayer today, we call on the words of Jesus on the cross: "Father, into your hands I commit my spirit." Resting in the Lord makes letting go of the difficult things in our lives at least possible, if not easy.

A SIMPLE GIFT

What emotional clutter is getting in your way? Sometimes we throw ourselves into the hectic pace of Christmas preparations for the very purpose of avoiding deeper issues. If you suspect that you might be doing this, take some time to pray about it and reflect on it. If you're not ready to deal with it at this time, promise yourself that you'll revisit it in the new year. You might find it helpful to talk to a professional or a trusted friend or you might be able to work on it yourself through prayer and journaling.

Be Grateful

How truly difficult it is to let ourselves be loved! We would always like a part of us to be freed of the debt of gratitude, while in reality we are completely indebted, because God loved us first and, with love, he saves us completely.

—POPE FRANCIS, HOMILY, MARCH 9, 2018

*W*hen you live alone, it's easy to fall into the delusion of self-sufficiency. Being independent and self-sufficient might be one of the myths of our twenty-first-century society, especially as we rely more and more on technology. But there are some things we can't google and there are even some things that Siri and Alexa can't do for us. Anyone who struggles with serious health issues has learned this lesson. It's those of us who are able-bodied and fiercely independent who need to be taught. And it's a lesson we don't learn willingly.

As I left to drive myself to the doctor last December, I knew I was leaving my four dogs without a caretaker. I left the doors of the house and the gate to the yard unlocked, but I hadn't made any other plans. Because I'd been sick for a few weeks, the house was a mess and the dishes hadn't been done. Given a choice, I wouldn't have invited anyone over for a visit until I had a chance to clean. But sometimes we don't have that choice. I had to let go of whatever uncomfortable feelings of pride and embarrassment were surfacing.

Once I was hooked up to oxygen and monitors and out of immediate danger, I had to give some thought to the creatures who depend on me for their very lives. Two friends from my Secular Franciscan fraternity came to get my keys to move my truck out of the doctor's parking lot. If I'm honest, I have to admit I'm possessive of my house, my truck, my belongings, in a way that is quite un-Franciscan. But circumstances forced me to let go of all that and trust that everything would work out fine.

I texted my neighbor who had watched the dogs when I was on vacation and asked her to let them out and feed them. I had to explain to her that I had a weird plumbing problem that involved emptying a bucket of water from the bathtub faucet into the toilet once a day because there was a hole in the bathtub drain and the faucet was leaking. And the doorknob on the front door had an annoying tendency to fall off when letting the dogs in and out. But Debbie not only looked after my beloved dogs, she did my dishes and cleaned up the clutter around my computer and came up to the hospital to visit me. She only asked that I fix the doorknob before the next time she needed to watch the dogs!

While all this was going on, I was struck by the thought that while part of me thought I should be horribly embarrassed by people going in and out of my house in the disordered state it was in, I was simply overwhelmed with gratitude for so many loving people in my life who were ready to step in and help me. One friend picked up my dog's eye drops, another brought me "proper tea." My nephew brought me a longer charger cord for my phone. A coworker came up with pizza one evening. A friend who was out of town on business sent a fresh fruit arrangement. Looking back on it even now, I feel immensely grateful. One of the nurses commented on how many visitors I had during the week.

Advent and Christmas are a time of gift-giving and hospitality. But sometimes we overlook the importance of receiving both gifts and help from others graciously and gratefully. It can be so much easier being the one doing the helping and the giving. I admitted to one of my friends recently that I find it almost impossible to ask for help. I could only admit this when I realized she had begun offering before I could ask.

The third Sunday of Advent is known as Gaudete Sunday, from the Latin word for "Rejoice." As we explore the theme of gratefulness this week, we will discover how much joy comes from the simple emotion of feeling grateful for the many ways God reaches out to us through others. And the more we know how much we are loved and appreciated, the more we can reach out to help others in turn.

DAY ONE

Rejoice in Goodness

Rejoice in the Lord always; again I will say, Rejoice. Let your gentleness be known to everyone. The Lord is near. Do not worry about anything, but in every-thing by prayer and supplication with thanksgiving let your requests be made known to God. And the peace of God, which surpasses all understanding, will guard your hearts and your minds in Christ Jesus.

—PHILIPPIANS 4:4–5

---

*M*ost of us want to be seen as strong and capable. We don't want to be helpless and needy. We fear vulnerability. Paul's advice to the Philippians is startling: "Let your gentle-ness be known to everyone." He's telling us that knowing God is near makes it safe to let our guard down. We don't trust others and often we don't even trust ourselves. If we've made bad choices in the past, we may not trust ourselves to make good choices. If we've been hurt, we instinctively protect ourselves from further harm. If our trust has been betrayed, we're reluctant to trust again. It's easy, even natural, to fall into these patterns of behavior.

The Scriptures tell us again and again not to be afraid. God's peace, Paul tells us, will guard our hearts and minds. Rejoicing in the Lord teaches us to see not only the times we have been hurt but also the many times we have been loved and sheltered and cherished. This season's gentle challenge is to dwell on the good things in our lives, the precious memories, the reminders of God's gracious love and mercy. It can be tempting to recall only the bad things in our past and to live in fear. But the Incarnation proclaims a return to the essential goodness in creation and in humanity.

Being grateful for all that is good in our lives gives us a secure place to stand and a reliable shelter when the storms of life rage around us. We need to remember, as a dear friend once told me, "Sometimes when the storm rages, God calms the storm. But sometimes God can only calm the child because the storm must continue to rage." Let yourself be calmed today.

TAKE A DEEP BREATH

Breathe in peace, breathe out anxiety. Breath in trust, breathe out worry. Ask God for what you need. Thank God for what you need! Let these words run through your mind: "The peace of God surpasses all understanding."

A SIMPLE GIFT

Our sensory memories play a big part in our moods. Take time to be grateful for the many ways you perceive the world around you—sight, sound, smell, and touch—and the people and places these perceptions evoke. Hang on to those that are most calming and find ways to keep them close.

DAY TWO

The Gift of Patience

Be patient, therefore, beloved, until the coming of the
Lord. The farmer waits for the precious crop from the
earth, being patient with it until it receives the early
and the late rains. You also must be patient. Strengthen
your hearts, for the coming of the Lord is near.

—JAMES 5:7–8

*P*atience can be in short supply at this time of year, when
everyone is too busy. Technology has speeded up our lives to
the point that we notice when our internet connection is slug-
gish or the person in front of us in the grocery checkout has too
many coupons. We don't even know why we're in such a hurry.
We've begun to value speed for its own sake.

And yet the things that really matter in life still take time and
patience. We can't speed up the growth of plants or animals
or babies. We can't speed up the time time it takes for healing,
whether it's our bodies or our spirits. And all of these things
are well worth the wait. Instead of hurrying, we need to find

ways to nurture ourselves and one another during the waiting time.

The refrain of Advent is "The Lord is near." Sometimes it's hard to believe this. We don't get the answers we want when we pray, or at least we don't get them immediately. This season can help us wrestle with the waiting time. While we wait for the perfection of the world in the second coming of Christ, we have the mystery of the Incarnation to guide us in making our world a little more ready. We can appreciate the small signs along the way to that perfect time and place.

TAKE A DEEP BREATH

People of earlier generations were far more aware of the slow growth of nature. We can learn a valuable lesson in patience from observing the small signs of growth. Take a walk today and notice not the bare branches of the trees but the terminal buds that signal next spring's leaves.

> For as the earth brings forth its shoots,
>   and as a garden causes what is sown in it to spring
>   up,

so the LORD God will cause righteousness and praise
to spring up before all the nations. (Isaiah 61:11)

A SIMPLE GIFT

Take time to notice. A friend mentioned a species of lily that
has no leaves. I mentioned that it was unfamiliar to me. Until
I was pulling into my driveway later that day and saw a bed
of the very same lilies in my neighbor's garden. A couple days
later, I saw the same flowers in two other yards on my street.
All it takes is a little attention.

DAY THREE
Don't Let Regret Hold You Back

"A man had two sons; he went to the first and said, 'Son, go and work in the vineyard today.' He answered, 'I will not'; but later he changed his mind and went. The father went to the second and said the same; and he answered, 'I go, sir'; but he did not go. Which of the two did the will of his father?" They said, "The first." Jesus said to them, "Truly I tell you, the tax-collectors and the prostitutes are going into the kingdom of God ahead of you. For John came to you in the way of righteousness and you did not believe him, but the tax-collectors and the prostitutes believed him; and even after you saw it, you did not change your minds and believe him."

—MATTHEW 21:28–32

*M*ost people know the parable of the prodigal son from Luke's Gospel. Matthew uses another story of two brothers to make a similar point. It doesn't have the elaborate details of

Luke's story, but sometimes that keeps us from being distracted from the central message.

I often find myself identifying with the actions of the younger son, to the point that I sometimes now tell people I'm working with that my tendency is to say no to something and then later come around to a yes response. I seem to need that time and space to consider what's being asked of me. And I believe that over time I will learn to temper that first response so that I can be more willing to reach out and say yes more quickly.

Because there's one more group of people that Jesus doesn't mention in his parable: those who say yes and follow through on their commitment. We all know these people in our lives, and we're grateful for their presence because they keep things moving and they're actively working to build up the kingdom. These are the people Pope Francis refers to as "the saints next door."

Gratitude teaches us how to come more quickly to a yes answer. It helps us live more easily in the present moment. Blessed Solanus Casey is quoted as saying, "We must be faithful to the present moment or we will frustrate the plan of God for our lives." This is good advice to those of who tend to live either in the past or the future. We need to notice what God is doing in and through us right here, right now.

TAKE A DEEP BREATH

Trust that you're going in the right direction and say yes to God's plan. Reflect on these words of St. Paul: "Keep on doing the things that you have learned and received and heard and seen in me, and the God of peace will be with you" (Philippians 4:6–7).

A SIMPLE GIFT

If you don't already have a gratitude journal, now might be the time to begin one. It doesn't need to be fancy. A plain spiral notebook will do, or even a sheet of paper. Many people do this before bed in the evening but you will settle on the time that works best for you. Writing these things down keeps them from being forgotten. If you're having a bad day, you can revisit your lists.

DAY FOUR
You Have Gifts to Offer

Shower, O heavens, from above,
>and let the skies rain down righteousness;
let the earth open, that salvation may spring up,
>and let it cause righteousness to sprout up also;
I the LORD have created it.

—ISAIAH 45:8

We've been trained from the time we were small children to say thank you for gifts, for compliments, for anything someone does for us. It's an excellent habit and goes a long way toward fostering an atmosphere of civility and goodwill. As we grow and mature, we learn to cultivate a deeper sense of gratitude beyond automatic words and gestures. It also breaks through the false humility that sometimes causes us to turn away compliments and deny our gifts. We discover the graciousness inherent in God's providence and we respond with a gratefulness that flows from us to all those around us.

Gratefulness teaches us that the things we have are meant

to be shared; the gifts particular to us are meant to enrich the world. The more we recognize our abundance, the more we want everyone to have that experience of grace and giftedness. And the more we share ourselves and our gifts with others, the more those gifts grow and develop.

This deep gratefulness is learned not so much from being told to be grateful as from watching those around us respond to the gifts in their own lives. When my mom, who was always generous to a fault, was struggling in the final days of her life, I found myself reminding her of all the ways she had reached out to her family through the years. I was stunned that she didn't recognize those gifts that were so apparent to those around her.

As we recognize and appreciate our own gifts, we teach others to do the same. It's good to have people in our lives who can remind us of this when we forget.

TAKE A DEEP BREATH

Reflect on this quote from Br. David Steindl-Rast: "The smallest surprise, received gratefully, yields a harvest of delight." Let your memory surface times in your life when you experienced this kind of delight. Think about how you might surprise someone else.

A SIMPLE GIFT

Be grateful for the gifts you bring to the lives of your loved ones. We often neglect this when we're taking a gratitude inventory.

DAY FIVE
Simple Presence

For the mountains may depart
  and the hills be removed,
but my steadfast love shall not depart from you,
  and my covenant of peace shall not be removed,
  says the LORD, who has compassion on you.

—ISAIAH 54:10

I'm sure for people living in Isaiah's time, the permanence of hills and mountains was something taken for granted. And so the prophet could suggest that God's steadfast love was even more solid and immovable than that. The reassurance is no less needed in these days when we know that both technology and nature can and do destroy mountains. The words of the prophet still ring true: God's love and compassion are with us in good times and bad.

We might think it's easier to recognize God's presence when life is good and happiness fills our spirits. We enjoy gathering with friends to celebrate the good times, the successes in our lives and theirs. But we know from experience that it's in the most difficult times in our lives that we are truly grateful for those who can simply be present to us in our fear, our anxiety, our sadness, and our grief. And it's in those times, too, that God's enfolding love surrounds us and keeps us going.

The holidays often bring with them a mix of emotions. We enjoy being with family and friends but few of us can say that we don't notice a tinge of sadness when we realize how many people we've lost over the years. This loss creeps up on us at the most unexpected times. It might be due to a variety of circumstances, not only death but also the transitory nature of modern life. Some of those people are only casual acquaintances but some have a deep impact on us and we feel the loss of their presence. As we remember them, it helps to thank God for bringing them into our lives.

TAKE A DEEP BREATH

Being happy doesn't make us grateful. Being grateful makes us happy. (Br. David Steindl-Rast)

As you focus on your breathing, reflect on the happy and sad times in your life. Let your mind and heart absorb the truth of this statement.

A SIMPLE GIFT

Be grateful for the simple presence of loved ones in your life. It's easy to be grateful for what people do for us or give to us, but their importance goes beyond this. Be grateful, too, for loved ones you have lost to death. Know that they are still very much present to you, even if it's in a very different way. Our grief is a measure of the depth of our love. If your grief is new and still raw, trust that it will become more gentle over time.

DAY SIX

Homecoming

And the foreigners who join themselves to the LORD,
    to minister to him, to love the name of the LORD,
    and to be his servants,
all who keep the sabbath, and do not profane it,
    and hold fast my covenant—
these I will bring to my holy mountain,
    and make them joyful in my house of prayer;
their burnt offerings and their sacrifices
    will be accepted on my altar;
for my house shall be called a house of prayer
    for all peoples.
Thus says the LORD God,
    who gathers the outcasts of Israel,
I will gather others to them
    besides those already gathered.

—ISAIAH 56:6–8

*B*eing grateful is a first small step toward not feeling guilty about the good things we have. As we realize that our lives are a gift, sometimes simply a gift of where and when we were born, we can let go of the defensiveness that leads us to believe we've earned and deserve what we have. But being grateful doesn't means simply being content with who we are and what we have. Nor is it a precursor to complacency. Being grateful makes us more aware of the people around us, those who have helped us but also those who need our help. Being grateful reminds us that we don't do anything entirely on our own.

Many of the great Hebrew prophets wrote to a people experiencing exile. At different times in our lives we may be able to identify with that experience. We might be stuck at home when we want to be out. We might be stuck at a party when we'd rather be at home with just one or two dearly loved friends. We might be in a job that keeps us far away from our families for long periods of time. When my mom was dying and trapped in a kind of emotional dementia, I discovered a whole new understanding of the line in the *Salve Regina* prayer that says, "And after this our exile…" I could see how much she was living in a kind of exile, away from the home and family she had known all her life and not yet in the eternal home with the God for whom she had longed all her life.

A true home is a place of inclusion and love where all are welcome, not a fortress to defend against the enemy. Our coming home challenges us to recognize that everyone is a child of the one God.

TAKE A DEEP BREATH

Through Isaiah, God says, "My house shall be called a house of prayer for all peoples." Let this be your prayer today.

A SIMPLE GIFT

Learn something new today about a person or group of people not like you in some way. Even acquiring a little knowledge about others brings us closer together. If you're feeling timid today, you can stick to simple research. If you're feeling brave or adventurous, make plans to meet with someone new. Remember the old saying that strangers are friends you haven't yet met.

DAY SEVEN
All Are Welcome

Therefore, the days are surely coming, says the LORD, when it shall no longer be said, "As the LORD lives who brought the people of Israel up out of the land of Egypt", but "As the LORD lives who brought out and led the offspring of the house of Israel out of the land of the north and out of all the lands where he had driven them." Then they shall live in their own land.

—JEREMIAH 23:7–8

*E*xodus and exile are among the most common themes in the Hebrew Scriptures. The Chosen People are driven from their homes and their land and God shelters them and leads them back home. While the Exodus is the founding experience for God's people, Jeremiah reminds his listeners that God will perform as great a rescue in their own lives. And from that day to this, this movement plays out in nations and in our own personal lives.

Yesterday we reflected on personal experiences of exile. Today we widen our perspective and give thought to those who are experiencing the kind of exile from their homelands that the people of Israel and the Holy Family in Egypt experienced. Our spiritual journey is never only about our own personal salvation. The prophets remind us that we are called to live our lives in such a way that the nations will find their way to God through us.

This perspective often challenges the status quo. In both the Old and New Testaments, exile happened because the leaders of the people and those who benefitted from a privileged existence forgot that they too had been lost and broken at one time and depended on God for their newfound good fortune. Our Scriptures remind us again and again that God will always side with the poor, the powerless, the broken. If we can't recognize this, if we think that being powerful is the way to find God, we are likely to be surprised. Any power and privilege we have is to be placed at the service of others.

TAKE A DEEP BREATH

The spirit of the LORD God is upon me,
   because the LORD has anointed me;
he has sent me to bring good news to the oppressed,
   to bind up the brokenhearted,
to proclaim liberty to the captives,
   and release to the prisoners;
to proclaim the year of the LORD's favor. (Isaiah 61:1–3)

A SIMPLE GIFT

The Scriptures, especially Luke's Gospel, place the birth of Jesus squarely in the middle of a very political setting. It's a reminder that our faith can't be something that sets us above and apart from the messiness of our world. As we become more grateful for the good things we have in our own lives, we want to share with those who have less. Find a group in your local community that is working to help refugees and immigrants and make an effort to contribute to their cause in some way.

Embrace the Mystery

*I*f we've celebrated Advent well, we come into this fourth week of Advent with a little more peace in our hearts, a little more centered calm in our souls. We have an anticipation that's not excited but not frenzied. If we're still searching for that peace, this is the time when it draws close. We come close to the simple, yet profound mystery at the heart of our faith: Our God took on human flesh and came to earth as a baby: needy, vulnerable, and utterly dependent on human parents in a small town in the Middle East.

The mystery of Christmas is anything but simple and yet it can be expressed in the simplest of ways. We take for granted the nativity scenes large and small that decorate our homes and churches. It was St. Francis who first had the idea of sharing the Christmas story through a live tableau on Christmas, emphasizing the humble and even poor setting for the birth of

Christ. Like the ordinary gifts of bread and wine that become the extraordinary body and blood of Christ at every Eucharist, the simplest gifts we share with one another can express our desire to love others as God has loved us.

When I got home from the hospital, my priorities had changed a great deal. I let go of much of the stress that had been weighing me down. Somehow none of the things I had been worrying about seemed so important anymore. I decided to visit my family in Wisconsin, surprising my sister for her sixty-fifth birthday. I focused on healing and finding better strategies for dealing with my chronic health issues. And I made a commitment to hang on to the things I'd discovered about myself and the God who loves and surprises me on such a frequent basis.

A friend and I were exchanging work stories one day. I knew how committed she was to the work she was doing and how she often focused on that work at the expense of anything else in her life. What surprised me was when she said, "You don't need your work. I get the sense that you have a kernel of self-worth that gives your life meaning no matter what." I knew she

Sell your books at sellbackyourBook.com!

Go to sellbackyourBook.com and get an instant price quote. We even pay the shipping - see what your old books are worth today!

00018278379

8379

was right, and I knew that it had been something I had been learning to cultivate over many years. And I was immensely grateful for it, because I knew that it freed me to make choices for my life more freely and honestly. But mostly it helped me keep all the demands of my life in balance.

The seasons of the liturgical year are more than markers on the calendar. They should change us as we experience the mysteries of our faith. In his book *The Holy Longing*, Fr. Ron Rolheiser talks about the way the paschal mystery reveals itself again and again in our own lives. If we are committed to modeling our lives on Christ's passion, death, and resurrection, we need to do these things: "Name our deaths, claim our births, grieve what we have lost and adjust to the new reality, not cling to the old but let it ascend to give its blessing, and accept the spirit of the life that we are already living." While Lent and Easter are the main celebration of the paschal mystery, Advent and Christmas also take part in that mystery. Birth and death mirror one another for people of faith. So do all the significant changes that happen throughout our lives.

In this final week of Advent, we journey with Elizabeth and Zechariah, with Mary and Joseph, as they respond to the life-changing events announced by the angel Gabriel. Our lives today may or may not be as dramatic, but we can learn from their faith—and their doubts—how to recognize and respond to the presence of God that's always revealing itself in our midst in new and familiar ways.

DAY ONE

God's Word Fulfilled

In those days Mary set out and went with haste to a Judean town in the hill country, where she entered the house of Zechariah and greeted Elizabeth. When Elizabeth heard Mary's greeting, the child leapt in her womb. And Elizabeth was filled with the Holy Spirit and exclaimed with a loud cry, "Blessed are you among women, and blessed is the fruit of your womb. And why has this happened to me, that the mother of my Lord comes to me? For as soon as I heard the sound of your greeting, the child in my womb leapt for joy. And blessed is she who believed that there would be a fulfillment of what was spoken to her by the Lord."

—LUKE 1:39–45

*A*ll the anticipation comes to a climax in this last week of Advent. From the early days of Advent when the focus is on the Second Coming at the end of time through the middle days when we reflect on the many ways God is present to us in our daily lives, we've arrived at the stories of the preparation for the coming of the Son of God as a baby in Bethlehem. The infinite and the intimate are both part of the wonder of Emmanuel.

Waiting might be one of the greatest challenges for modern people. It's woven into so much of what we do, and as we've seen, it required both patience and trust. Waiting for birth and waiting for death (itself a rebirth into eternity) might be the most intense times of waiting we experience. Rushing either one does irreparable damage to the web of life.

Elizabeth exclaims to Mary, "Blessed is she who believed that there would be a fulfilment of what was spoken to her by the Lord." One wonder whether her blessing is for Mary or herself or more likely for both. Because each woman heard a promise that seemed almost impossible and yet she chose to trust in the wisdom and power of God to bring that promise to fulfillment. Their journey isn't over at this point, but as they join in celebration of that promise, the road is made easier by the presence of a companion on the way.

We need to recover and reignite the power of blessing in our lives. It's a way of making holy both the ordinary and extraordinary moments in our lives. In blessing ourselves and one another we acknowledge the presence of God in our midst.

TAKE A DEEP BREATH

Meditation is nothing new for Catholics. We may have called it by different names through our long history, but the pattern of quiet reflection on the divine mystery and prayers to help our busy minds find focus is deeply rooted in our spiritual tradition. Take time today to pray the joyful mysteries of the rosary. Today's Gospel is the second of those, the visitation of Mary to Elizabeth.

A SIMPLE GIFT

At night before you go to bed, make a conscious effort to ask God to bless those near and dear to you. I remember once seeing my grandma sprinkling holy water in the air in her bedroom and I knew instinctively that she was blessing each of us. You might also want to begin to say, "God bless you" when you say, "I love you."

DAY TWO
Blessed Silence

Then there appeared to him an angel of the Lord, standing at the right side of the altar of incense. When Zechariah saw him, he was terrified; and fear overwhelmed him. But the angel said to him, "Do not be afraid, Zechariah, for your prayer has been heard. Your wife Elizabeth will bear you a son, and you will name him John. You will have joy and gladness, and many will rejoice at his birth, for he will be great in the sight of the Lord...." Zechariah said to the angel, "How will I know that this is so? For I am an old man, and my wife is getting on in years." The angel replied, "I am Gabriel. I stand in the presence of God, and I have been sent to speak to you and to bring you this good news."

—LUKE 1:11–14, 18–20

Zechariah and Elizabeth prayed throughout their married lives for the Lord to bless them with children. To have those prayers answered when it seemed far too late for them to be fulfilled must have seemed at first like a cruel joke, a message that was too little and too late. We can understand Zechariah's doubting the angel's word. Even if Elizabeth bore a child at such an advanced age, he couldn't imagine seeing that child grow up and fulfill the destiny promised by the angel. In spite of the face that he had been a holy priest all his life, serving daily in the Temple, this promise seemed too far beyond his ability to believe.

It may have been a relief for Zechariah and Elizabeth to withdraw from the busyness of Temple life for a time, he in his imposed silence, she in the wonder of the new life growing in her womb. In the face of great mystery, silence might be the only authentic response. And too often the chatter of outsiders and the gossip of those who only half understand what's going on can be wearing and stressful.

We live in a world where the most intimate sides of people's lives can be broadcast to the world, with or without their consent. We forget that everyone has a right to privacy and personal time away from prying eyes and babbling gossip. This isn't a new phenomenon, but technology has vastly enlarged the concept of the village gossip.

The pain of infertility is something that many people struggle with, often privately and silently. We need to guard against making assumptions (even judgments) about couples with no children. Allow people to share the intimate details of their lives if and when they choose. There are many good and personal reasons for choosing to raise children, just as there here are many other ways to be fruitful and life-giving. Sometimes silence is indeed golden.

TAKE A DEEP BREATH

Read the story of the announcement of the birth of John the Baptist (Luke 1:5–25) and reflect on the many emotions the characters must have experienced. What memories from your own life does this story awaken?

A SIMPLE GIFT

Limit your exposure to the news during the week before Christmas. We don't realize how overwhelming our 24/7 news broadcasts can be. Even the local broadcasts morning, noon, and night come into our homes with a constant repetition of bad news that often has no real meaning for our lives beyond a salacious appeal to our curiosity. Christmas is a time to rejoice in the good news of the many wondrous things that God has done and will continue to do.

DAY THREE
Nothing Is Impossible with God

The angel said to her, "The Holy Spirit will come upon
you, and the power of the Most High will overshadow
you; therefore the child to be born will be holy; he will
be called Son of God. And now, your relative Elizabeth
in her old age has also conceived a son; and this is the
sixth month for her who was said to be barren. For
nothing will be impossible with God." Then Mary
said, "Here am I, the servant of the Lord; let it be with
me according to your word."

—LUKE 1:35–38

Luke weaves together the annunciation and birth of John
the Baptist and the annunciation and birth of Jesus. The first is
marvelous but still comprehensible in human terms. John, the
precursor, was born of human parents, conceived in the normal
way (if a bit past the normal age for begetting). Zechariah and
Gabriel have something of a confrontation of wills. This isn't
unusual in the Hebrew Scriptures, where quite a few characters

wrestle and argue with their divine messengers. With Mary, the scene ascends out of the earthly realm into something that had never happened before or since. She's perplexed, she questions, but she doesn't doubt. This might be the greatest sign of her special grace and favor. Mary, filled with God's grace, says yes. And that yes changed the human race and creation for all time.

We can barely imagine what this experience must have been like for Mary: to be chosen, out of all the women in history, to bear the Son of God, the Messiah long promised to her people. It is indeed a singular experience. But each of us is favored by God and called to bring forth a bit of divine life in our own place and time. And it might seem as overwhelming as Mary's call was to her. God doesn't tell us not to question, but rather not to be afraid. And whether we come to our response as slowly as Zechariah or as quickly as Mary, we do come to it in the end. And with God's grace, that answer will be yes.

TAKE A DEEP BREATH

Hear the words of the angel Gabriel spoken in your heart: "Greetings, favored one! The Lord is with you.... Do not be afraid...for you have found favor with God" (see Luke 1:28–30). What is your initial reaction? Turn the words over a time or two. What comes to mind? What do you think the Lord might be asking of you? Breathe deeply. How does your response change? What will you do next?

A SIMPLE GIFT

We all know people who are dealing with seemingly impossible situations on their lives. Send a special card to someone who is struggling through a particularly rough patch right now. If you're an archangel, you can simply declare that nothing is impossible with God. If you're a finite human being, the words can ring hollow; you need to find a concrete and compassionate way to convey this message. Sometimes it means simply being present to another person, holding them in prayer, letting them know they're loved in the midst of their struggles. Sometimes it's taking action with and for them. Trust God to give you the words and show you the way.

DAY FOUR
Renewed in God's Love

The LORD, your God, is in your midst,
  a warrior who gives victory;
he will rejoice over you with gladness,
  he will renew you in his love;
he will exult over you with loud singing
  as on a day of festival.
I will remove disaster from you,
  so that you will not bear reproach for it.

                  —ZEPHANIAH 3:17–18

*L*uke masterfully brings together the main characters in his first chapter when Mary, newly pregnant, goes to visit Elizabeth. Everyone reads something different into this visit. Was she going to help her elderly cousin at a difficult time? Did she want to prove the truth of Gabriel's message? Was she afraid her immediate family would reject her? I like to think her first impulse was, "Here is someone who will truly understand what I'm experiencing."

Mary and Elizabeth exclaim over the incredible events taking place in their lives. They sing with joy in the long tradition of their faith. Mary's words echo those of Hannah, another woman who was miraculously with child. In times of great joy as well as times of crisis, being able to gather with another or others who share that experience is a great comfort.

One of our deepest longings as human beings, as social beings, is to be understood even (or perhaps especially) in our most perplexing and difficult moments. We long to be loved for who we are, with the worst of our shortcomings and the best of our gifts. We want people in our lives who will rejoice with us, who will weep with us, who will simply be present to us. In these moments of deep connection with one another, we truly experience the presence of God in our midst, renewing us in his love. This is the promise of the prophets, a promise that came to fulfillment in the Incarnation.

TAKE A DEEP BREATH

The great mystery of Christmas, of the Incarnation, is that the infinite and the intimate move back and forth in our souls all the time. In our most intense human experiences, we touch the divine. Spend some time in prayer today reflecting on this quote. What experiences and memories come to mind as part of your reflection?

> By means of all created things, without exception, the divine assails us, penetrates us, and molds us. We imagined it as distant and inaccessible, when in fact we live steeped in its burning layers." (Pierre Teilhard de Chardin)

A SIMPLE GIFT

Who is the first person you call (or text) when you have something significant to share? How does sharing your joy, your sorrow, your confusion, your elation, intensify the experience? How does it bring you comfort and a feeling of being understood? Make sure you let that person know how important they are to you.

DAY FIVE

Because She Said Yes

From Mary the Church has acquired and constantly acquires this inner perception of fullness, which fosters a sense of gratitude, as a unique human response worthy of the immense Gift of God. A heartrending gratitude which, beginning from the contemplation of that Child swaddled and laid in a manger, extends to everything and to everyone, to the entire world.

—POPE FRANCIS, VESPERS AT THE END OF THE YEAR,
DECEMBER 31, 2017

*F*illed with God's grace, Mary knew who she was to the very depth of her being. She said yes to God and because of that, the world was turned upside down, or perhaps was finally righted. Mary's is her testimony to the way God intended the world to be from the beginning. Because she said yes, a new creation would be revealed to the world.

This woman at the heart of the Advent season is a remarkable role model for us. We might not realize it, but we, too, are filled with God's grace, even if that grace is clouded and obscured by sin. Mary may have been born knowing who she was, but we are given many opportunities to learn the marvelous truth that we are sons and daughters of God. At times, we mistake humility for inferiority, but in truth humility means knowing who we are, with all our strengths and weaknesses, gifts and gaps. Our job is to clear away those things that keep us from saying yes to God. If we focus only on what's missing, we miss the beauty that's already there.

As we become more and more clear, we better reflect and magnify the Lord who has given us all that we have, made us all that we are (and can be). And here, too, we can learn from Mary. Again and again, the Gospels tell us that she treasured everything in her heart, pondering the meaning of the angel's words—and later those of her precocious child. She must have spent long days and even sleepless nights wondering where his adult path would lead him. But through all of ponderings, she knew in her heart that she could trust the God to whom she had said yes.

TAKE A DEEP BREATH

How do you show forth the glory of God to those around you?
Pray these words with Mary:

> My soul magnifies the Lord,
>   and my spirit rejoices in God my Savior.
> (Luke 1:46–47)

A SIMPLE GIFT

We'll never be asked to do what Mary did. Her role in salvation history was unique. But God asks us to have her openness to those things that we are called to do. Take some time even in this hectic week to reflect on your life—past, present, and future—and listen for how God is asking you to make things right in your little corner of the world.

DAY SIX
Our Hopes and Dreams

And you, child, will be called the prophet of the Most
  High;
  for you will go before the Lord to prepare his ways,
to give knowledge of salvation to his people
  by the forgiveness of their sins.
By the tender mercy of our God,
  the dawn from on high will break upon us,
to give light to those who sit in darkness and in the
  shadow of death,
  to guide our feet into the way of peace.

—LUKE 1:76–79

We all have hopes and dreams for the children in our lives.
Whether it's starting a college fund the day they're born or
simply praying that they will be healthy and happy, we want
what's best for them. These dreams are surely the most idyllic
when children are infants, before they learn the word *no*. And

our hopes can be battered and bruised through the years by all kinds of unforeseen circumstances.

When Zechariah proclaims not only his hopes for his son, John, but God's plan, he gives words to every parent's deepest hope that their children will make a positive difference in the world. And if Zechariah lived long enough to see John grow to adulthood, he must have wondered often whether this original hope would come to fruition. Few parents envision their children dressed in camel hair and preaching in the desert. And John's murder at the hands of a narcissistic king must have seemed like the final blow. But John did, in fact, fulfill God's plan for his life. He led people to recognize the Christ, the Messiah, the anointed one.

It's easy to see the people in Scripture as far removed from our lives. Like any good story, we get to read the ending, we see how it all turns out for them. Our stories are mostly still unfinished. We might be struggling right now to see God's plan unfolding, whether in our own lives or those of our children. But Christmas is the beginning of the ultimate happy ending.

TAKE A DEEP BREATH

Sit with these words from Zechariah's canticle. If you find yourself in darkness, let them bring you hope. If you're seeing the sunrise, rejoice and give thanks!

By the tender mercy of our God,
the dawn from on high will break upon us...

A SIMPLE GIFT

Bless the children in your life today, whatever their ages, wherever they are. Trust that at the deepest heart of your hopes and dreams for them is God's own hopes and dreams for their lives, because they're God's sons and daughters as well.

DAY SEVEN
Open Wide the Doors

In the Child of Bethlehem, God comes to meet us and make us active sharers in the life around us. He offers himself to us, so that we can take him into our arms, lift him and embrace him…. In this Child, God invites us to be messengers of hope. He invites us to become sentinels for all those bowed down by the despair born of encountering so many closed doors. In this child, God makes us agents of his hospitality.

—POPE FRANCIS, HOMILY ON THE NATIVITY, DECEMBER 24, 2017

The simple yet profound mystery of the Incarnation is this: The Word of God became flesh and made his dwelling among us. Scripture scholars tell us that this phrase in John's Gospel literally translates as "pitched his tent" with his people. Like God's presence in the Ark of the Covenant, as the Chosen People traveled through the desert, so now God would come to earth as a vulnerable but graced infant, getting the same start in life that each and every one of us has.

Our God wants to be with us wherever we are. No dwelling is too lowly, no circumstances too humble. St. Francis recognized this when he created the first live nativity scene at Greccio: a cave, some animals, a deep faith in God's promise. And tradition tells us that he held the baby in his arms during the Mass.

We probably celebrate hospitality more at Christmas than we do at any other time of the year. We host parties, we attend parties, we revel in food and drink and presents. We also open not only our hearts but our wallets to those in need. It's a blessing to be able to do this. Maybe this is the year that we decide to carry this spirit of hospitality forward into the rest of the year, to become God's sentinels of hope. God comes into our lives, into our homes, into our world every day in many different disguises. Pope Francis reminds us that Christmas calls us to be on the lookout for this manifestation of the divine. And if God wants to dwell with us, we better be willing to open our doors to him.

TAKE A DEEP BREATH

Breathe in the vast spirit of Christmas today and throughout the Christmas season.

Do not be afraid! Open, open wide the doors to Christ! (St. John Paul II)

A SIMPLE GIFT

Celebrate well with your family and friends. Share what you've discovered about yourself during this Advent season. Let them see the changes God has brought about in your life. If we've been changed by Advent this year, we will be ready to move out of ourselves once more and reach out to others.

The Silence of Advent

Advent calls us to seek the grace of winter
   in silence and in hope.
   Early evening journeys into night.
   Branches etched against a garnet and sapphire sunset reveal
      a structure strong yet delicate.
   The symmetry suggests reflection . . . contemplation . . . inner
      peace.
   Advent reveals our own inner strength and the fragility of
      our hearts,
   as we learn to put our faith in what really matters.
   As darkness deepens, the branches fade to black.
   Stars glitter hard and white against the sky.
Advent comes into the darkness of our lives with the promise
   of light
   as we reflect on who we are and who we follow.

   Lights glow in windows along the road, calling us to warmth
      and comfort—

generous gifts from God through one another.

Advent holds out to us a love born of risk and vulnerability, of
compassion and security.

As we begin our journey through the darkness of Advent,
the promise of God's love lights our way.

May dawn find us rejoicing.

Advent calls us into the winter of the year to see the beauty
of waiting—

darkness waiting for light, silence waiting for a song, hearts
waiting for love.

Advent calls us to a deep inner conversion.

Along the way, the light fades and we feel our determination
wearing thin.

We want to rest, to quit. We don't want to hurt anymore.

We wait . . . and wait . . . and wait.

We hope and despair in turn.

We cling to whatever comfort and reassurance we can find.

But through it all we grow.

And we discover the promise of new life where we never
imagined it.

In the dark silence, when our lives are uncertain,
  we discover people who stay with us in our confusion,
  people who remind us of the promise,
  people who believe in us when we struggle to believe in
    ourselves.
We find people who walk with us in our winter journeys,
who call us to be faithful when we're drifting,
who hold us when we need to be held.

In the silence of Advent, we're set free from our fears...and
  we set others free.
We no longer need to be afraid of the dark,
  whether it be the darkness of the world around us
  or the darkness of the shadows within our hearts.

In the silence of exile, the prophet Zephaniah
  speaks words of encouragement and reassurance, to his
    people.
He shows them a vision of a God who rejoices over them,
who renews them in love,

who sings joyfully because of them.
We need not be discouraged, need not fear misfortune, held
    as we are in God's love.
No one can take away the pain of being human.
But God will come to us in the darkness
with soothing lullabies and a promise of dawn.

In the silence of Advent, we let ourselves dream of love.
We touch the longings and the hopes that lie deep within us.
Letting ourselves love and be loved is one of the greatest risks
    we ever take.
And we can't begin to love until the word of God whispers
    to us in the silence
that we are loved beyond belief, beyond telling.

In the silence of Advent, we hear,
"You are loved and lovable, simply because God has created
    you."
This love calls us to be gentle, to give of ourselves,
to grow and to change, above all to trust.

It calls us to conversion with compassion and gentleness;
it molds us without breaking us.

In the silence of Advent,
we come to know that no real love can be born without risks,
    without vulnerability.
When words fail, we reach out to one another in touch.
A loving embrace communicates what hours of conversation
    have left unsaid.
Somewhere in the depths of an Advent love, words give way
to the fullness of silence and sacrament.

And then, out of the silence of Advent comes a sense of
    anticipation and wonder.
God's love awakens within us a deep faith in promises made,
    kept, broken, reconciled.
Out of the silence of Advent comes the promise of the
    Incarnation.
"The Word was made flesh and dwelt among us."
God's passion for creation was at last a flesh-and-blood
    reality.

Out of the silence of Mary's womb, a baby emerged into a
  world of human struggle.
The infant, born in a stable in Bethlehem, outgrew the
  manger in which he was laid
and the swaddling bands in which he was wrapped,
as he would later leave the tomb and throw off the
  wrappings of death.
Jesus of Nazareth grew up to challenge his world and ours
with the promise of everlasting love.
With his hands, he offered a healing touch;
with his arms, he held and consoled;
with his feet, he walked with his friends and disciples.
And after all was said and done he offered his very body and
  blood.
The Word was consumed in the wordless eloquence of the
  cross and the silence of the empty tomb.

Out of that silence is raised a passionate belief in promise, in
  covenant.
When despair overwhelms us, when promises suddenly seem
  empty,

when it seems that we're surrounded by dashed dreams and
    disappointment,
by love betrayed and friendships faltering,
we remember that we've staked our lives on the belief that
    only through death is there life.

Out of the silence, we must go forth and proclaim the love of
    God alive and dwelling in our midst.
To this love we commit all that we are and all that we can
    become.
We follow Jesus of Nazareth. We love as he loved.
And so we are called to bring a healing touch to those who
    hurt,
to gather people into a loving embrace,
to cry out at the horrors of oppression and destruction,
to cherish the gifts of creation in all its varied forms.

We must become the word of love spoken by God in our
    hearts.
We must become the Good News made flesh for our world.

—Diane M. Houdek, 1986